THE HOLOCAUST

THE ORIGINS, EVENTS, AND REMARKABLE TALES OF SURVIVAL

PHILIP STEELE

The Hall of Names at the Yad Vashem Museum, Jerusalem, Israel. This cone-shaped memorial contains photographs of 600 people who died during the Holocaust.

CONTENTS

INTRODUCTION

In most schools today, it is the teacher's job to stop bullying. In Germany in the 1930s, it was often the teacher who was the bully. He would call Jewish pupils to the front of the class and order them to stand with their heads bowed while he mocked them and wrote on the blackboard, "The Jew is our Greatest Enemy."

Incidents like these were part of a wave of **discrimination** and **persecution** that evolved into the **Holocaust**—the catastrophic murder of millions of Jews and other peoples by the Nazi **regime** in Germany and its **collaborators**. The Nazis, who came to power in Germany in 1933, believed that the Germans were part of a white "master race," and that black people, Asians, Slavs, and others were lower forms of life. They particularly hated the Jews. They called them *Untermenschen*, which means "subhumans."

After World War II broke out in 1939, Germany invaded much of Western, Central, and Eastern Europe. Nazi persecution spread across Europe. Jews were rounded up and imprisoned in camps. They were starved, forced into hard labor, tortured, and even made to undergo medical experiments. By the spring of 1942, the Nazis' **"Final Solution** to the Jewish Question"** had taken shape. After that date, the Nazis and their collaborators organized the mass murder of Jews from all over Europe.

This dark period of human history later became known as the Holocaust. This word comes from the Ancient Greek for burning an animal as a sacrifice to the gods. It later came to mean a great massacre or slaughter. Another term for this period is the Shoah, from the Hebrew word for "catastrophe."

About six million Jews were killed by the Nazis, along with about five million others—Roma and Sinti (Gypsies), Slavs, disabled people, homosexuals, Soviet **prisoners of war**, and religious groups who opposed the Nazis.

The attempted extinction of a whole people is called **genocide**. The Holocaust was neither the first nor the last genocide in the world, but its chilling scale and nature of the killing marked it as one of the most appalling and barbaric events in human history.

PART 1: THE COMING STORM

Europe has a long history of civilization and concern for **human rights**. It has shaped some of the basic ideas behind **democratic** government. But it also has a darker history of **oppression**, political violence, and **racism**. Jewish, Roma, and other communities have often been persecuted. At the start of the twentieth century, Europeans had new opportunities that their ancestors could only have dreamed of. However, such dreams faded as war and economic hardship created fear and suffering. The destruction and instability caused by World War I (1914–1918) enabled extreme parties, such as the Nazi party in Germany, to take control. A new wave of racism evolved that challenged our deepest beliefs in human nature.

The devastated landscape of a battlefield in Belgium, Northern Europe, after World War I.

9

JEWISH ROOTS

TODAY, JEWS LIVE ALL AROUND THE WORLD, BUT THEIR ORIGINS ARE IN SOUTHWEST ASIA. THEIR ANCESTORS FOUNDED A KINGDOM, SOMETIMES REFERRED TO AS THE UNITED MONARCHY, OVER 3,000 YEARS AGO. THIS LATER DIVIDED INTO THE SEPARATE KINGDOMS OF ISRAEL AND JUDAH.

Hebrew scriptures (religious texts) describe how the Jews are descended from a patriarch, or founding father, called Abraham. For centuries, the Jews were under threat from the powerful warring empires of the region—the Egyptian, Assyrian, Babylonian, Persian, Greek, and Roman empires. The Jews suffered periods of exile, slavery, conquest, and revolt. Many Jews left their homeland.

BRITAIN

FRANCE

SPAIN

THE DIASPORA

The dispersal of a people to other lands is called a **"diaspora."** Over thousands of years, Jews settled across the Middle East, North Africa, parts of Europe—including Spain and Germany —and eventually the Americas. The scattered communities developed varying customs and traditions. Jews in **medieval** Spain and Portugal were known as Sephardim, while those in Germany were known as Ashkenazim.

NORTH AFRICA

The Torah, or Jewish Law, is a religious text traditionally written on a parchment scroll in Hebrew.

JEWISH LANGUAGES

The ancient language of the Jews was Hebrew. Later, Hebrew was used mostly as a language of religion, but was revived as an everyday language in modern times. Other languages spoken by Jews in the ancient world included Aramaic. Local languages were spoken throughout the diaspora. From the 10th century, the Ashkenazim developed their own Germanic language, called Yiddish. The Sephardim also developed a language, called Ladino or Judesmo.

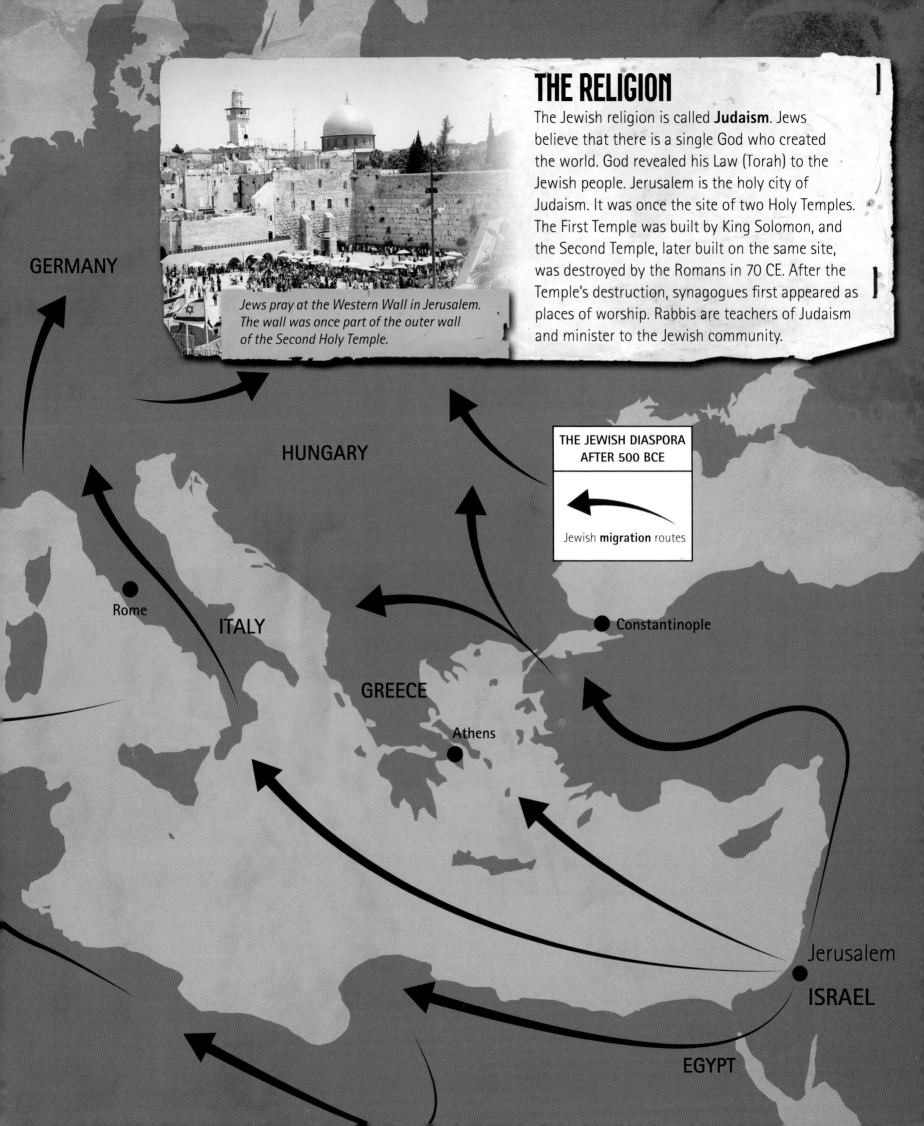

THE RELIGION

The Jewish religion is called **Judaism**. Jews believe that there is a single God who created the world. God revealed his Law (Torah) to the Jewish people. Jerusalem is the holy city of Judaism. It was once the site of two Holy Temples. The First Temple was built by King Solomon, and the Second Temple, later built on the same site, was destroyed by the Romans in 70 CE. After the Temple's destruction, synagogues first appeared as places of worship. Rabbis are teachers of Judaism and minister to the Jewish community.

Jews pray at the Western Wall in Jerusalem. The wall was once part of the outer wall of the Second Holy Temple.

GERMANY

HUNGARY

THE JEWISH DIASPORA AFTER 500 BCE

Jewish **migration** routes

Rome

ITALY

● Constantinople

GREECE

Athens

Jerusalem

ISRAEL

EGYPT

THE JEWS IN EUROPE

THE JEWISH COMMUNITIES THAT DEVELOPED IN EUROPE WERE OFTEN THRIVING CENTERS OF **CULTURE** AND LEARNING. IN THE LATER MIDDLE AGES (c.1000–1500 CE), JEWS BECAME FAMOUS FOR THEIR SKILLS AS DOCTORS, SCIENTISTS, POETS, AND FINANCIERS. During this period, there were times when communities flourished as people from the three faiths of Judaism, **Islam,** and Christianity lived peacefully side by side. However, there were setbacks, too, when religious strife destroyed goodwill among people of different faiths.

A wood engraving depicting market day in a Jewish district of a Dutch town in the 1860s.

MAIMONIDES THE SCHOLAR

Moshe ben Maimon, or Maimonides, was a distinguished Jew who is famous for his work in medicine, astronomy, philosophy, and linguistics. He was born in the city of Córdoba, Spain, in 1135, during a time when its rulers were followers of Islam. He served as a rabbi in Egypt and Morocco and became the court doctor to the sultan Saladin, the famous Islamic military leader. In 1171, he became head of the Jewish community in Egypt. His writings on medicine and philosophy have influenced Jewish and non-Jewish scholars alike.

A statue of Maimonides stands in the old Jewish Quarter of Córdoba, Spain.

12

INTOLERANCE TOWARD THE JEWS

Judaism, Christianity, and Islam have much in common. They all originate from Southwest Asia and worship a single God. All three faiths mention the Jewish patriarch Abraham and the leader Moses in their religious texts. But throughout history, Christians often ignored the fact that Jesus himself was Jewish. Some Christians blamed the Jews rather than the Romans for Jesus's death. During the later Middle Ages, the Roman Catholic Church's **intolerance** of other religions grew stronger. Jews were often singled out for vicious attacks. They were expelled from European cities and states, forced to convert to Christianity, and attacked and killed.

In the 15th and 16th centuries, Jews and others who refused to become Roman Catholics were sometimes executed by burning.

This engraving shows a riot against Jews in Frankfurt-am-Main, Germany, in 1819.

GHETTOS AND POGROMS

Jews fled from persecution, or unfair treatment, in medieval Spain and England to more tolerant places, such as the city of Amsterdam, in the Netherlands. In Germany and Eastern Europe, violent attacks on Jewish communities were also common. In some cities, such as Venice, Rome, Prague, and Frankfurt-am-Main, laws were passed that confined the Jews to special city districts called **ghettos**. In the 1800s and 1900s, brutal attacks on Jewish communities in the Russian Empire became known as **pogroms**.

JEWS IN MODERN CIVILIZATION

As Jews took part in wider European society, some chose (or were forced) to abandon their religion. Despite persecution, people of Jewish descent helped to shape the history and culture of modern Europe. They included the painter Marc Chagall (1887-1985) and classical music composers such as Felix Mendelssohn (1809-1847) and Gustav Mahler (1860-1911). Benjamin Disraeli (1804-1881) served as a prime minister of Great Britain and Ireland, and Karl Marx (1818-1883) was a great German economist and political thinker. Albert Einstein (1879-1955) was one of the greatest scientists in history.

Marc Chagall's famous painting "The Fiddler" depicts a musician from the artist's hometown of Vitebsk, Russia, which had a large population of Jews.

13

GERMANY AFTER WORLD WAR I

Defeated German soldiers are marched through the devastated landscape of World War I.

IN THE 1880s AND 90s, MANY EUROPEANS WERE HOPEFUL ABOUT THE WORLD'S FUTURE. THEY HAD LIVED THROUGH ADVANCES IN SCIENCE AND IN **SOCIAL JUSTICE**. BUT IN 1914 SUCH HOPES WERE SHATTERED BY THE OUTBREAK OF WORLD WAR I.

During World War I, in four years of the worst bloodshed yet known in history, the Central Powers (Germany, Austria–Hungary, and the Ottoman Empire) battled with the Allies (Britain, France, Russia, Italy, and Japan), who were joined in 1917 by the United States.

GERMANY IN TURMOIL

Germany was defeated in November 1918. This defeat led to **mutiny**, starvation, and social unrest. There were uprisings in Germany by political activists called **communists**, some of whom were Jewish. They were inspired by a communist **revolution** that had swept Russia in 1917. The revolutionaries were attacked and defeated on the streets by armed groups known as the *Freikorps*. The *Freikorps* included many embittered former soldiers who were eager to blame others for their defeat in World War I.

A recruitment poster for the Freikorps. It reads "Protect your homeland! Enlist in the Freikorps."

14

A HARSH PEACE

The terms of the peace between Germany and the Allies were drawn up in Paris, but Germany was not included in the discussions. The result of the conference was the Treaty of Versailles (1919). The Allies wanted to make sure that Germany could not go to war again. It lost some of its territories and had its military forces reduced. The Allies also demanded huge sums of money called **reparations** from the Germans. Some people wondered if this was the settling of one conflict, or the road to another.

A painting showing the signing of the Treaty of Versailles in 1919, by the artist William Orpen (1878-1931).

THE WEIMAR REPUBLIC

In 1919 a new German state was proclaimed in the city of Weimar. This was to be a modern democratic government. The Weimar **Republic** took steps to reduce the harsh terms of the Versailles treaty, but it was not able to stabilize German politics or the economy. The government was made up of several small political parties unable to agree on policies and pass laws effectively. In 1920, there was a rebellion known as the Kapp Putsch. It failed, but helped to further destabilize the government.

Supporters of the Kapp Putsch march through Berlin, Germany, in 1920.

THE LEAGUE OF NATIONS

An international treaty organization called the League of Nations was founded in 1920 to make the world a more peaceful place. It was an earlier version of today's United Nations (UN), but it lacked political power, partly because it failed to get the backing of the United States Senate. The League proved to be unable to stop the coming of another war or protect the Jewish people from the persecution that was to follow.

The first meeting of the League of Nations in Geneva, Switzerland, in 1920.

HARD TIMES BREED HATRED

GERMANY HAD PAID FOR WORLD WAR I BY BORROWING MONEY AND, AS A RESULT, HAD HUGE DEBTS. NOW IT ALSO HAD TO PAY EXTRA MONEY IN REPARATIONS TO THE VICTORIOUS COUNTRIES.

With no reserves of money, Germany had to pay with precious raw materials, such as coal. Germany's main industrial region, the Ruhr, was **occupied** by French soldiers. The German economy could not recover. The former Allies drew up various plans to ease the pressure, but these failed.

This photograph shows children making a kite out of German mark banknotes. Spiraling prices had made the money almost worthless.

Prices rose so high that banknotes worth a million or even a billion German marks had to be printed.

MONEY MADNESS

When the costs of goods and services rise over a period of time, it is called **inflation**. Between 1921 and 1924, Germany experienced extreme inflation. As prices soared, the currency could buy less and less. By 1923, one American dollar was worth 4,210,500,000,000 German marks. Germans had to carry a suitcase full of banknotes just to buy a loaf of bread. The chaos weakened the power of the government and made it unpopular.

BROOKLYN DAILY EAGLE
And Complete Long Island News

WALL ST. IN PANIC AS STOCKS CRAS

Attempt Made to Kill Italy's Crown Prince

The Wall Street Crash makes headlines in a New York newspaper on October 24, 1929.

THE DEPRESSION YEARS

Germany's economic troubles were made worse when the financial system of other powerful industrial countries also weakened. In 1929, the value of shares being traded on the New York Stock Exchange crashed. Fortunes were lost overnight and banks closed. This "Wall Street Crash" was the start of a long economic downturn called the Great Depression, which affected most of the world. International trade slowed down as factories were closed. By 1932, thirty percent of the German workforce was unemployed.

ANGER AND BLAME

The economic problems played into the hands of extreme political groups such as the National Socialist German Workers' Party, which was founded in 1920. Its supporters, known as Nazis, stirred up public feelings against the Weimar government and the Versailles treaty, calling for Germany to rebuild its military might. They said they would create jobs. They blamed banks, big business, and communists for the troubles—but soon they also directed the public anger against Jewish companies.

People hit by the economic hardship had to make use of soup kitchens, such as this one in Berlin.

"We have no butter . . . but I ask you, would you rather have butter or guns? Preparedness makes us powerful. Butter merely makes us fat."

Hermann Goering, leading member of the Nazi Party, January 17, 1936

THE RISE OF THE NAZIS

AFTER WORLD WAR I, THERE WAS SUPPORT FOR EXTREME **NATIONALIST** POLITICAL PARTIES IN SEVERAL EUROPEAN COUNTRIES, INCLUDING SPAIN, GREECE, AUSTRIA, POLAND, THE UNITED KINGDOM, AND FRANCE.

These parties embraced national unity and used military uniforms and symbols. Many of them took their lead from the National **Fascist** Party, founded in Italy in 1921. Some of them remained small, but others came to power. It took the Nazi Party only thirteen years to win control of Germany.

Thousands of people poured into the main square in Munich in 1923 when the Nazis tried to seize power.

GUNS OR VOTES?

The Nazis first came to public notice in 1923, when they tried unsuccessfully to seize power with an armed uprising in the city of Munich. Their leader, Adolf Hitler, was imprisoned for a short time. The Nazis also took part in elections, because Hitler wanted to be seen as respectable. In reality, the Nazis also used street violence, intimidation, and bullying to win votes.

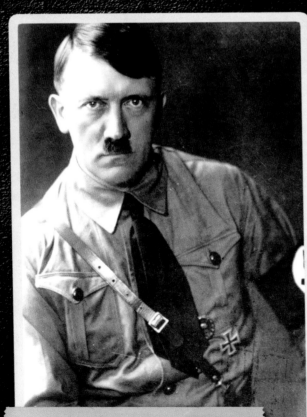

Adolf Hitler in Nazi uniform in 1932. He become known as the Führer, or leader.

ADOLF HITLER

Adolf Hitler was born in 1889 in Austria and fought in World War I. He became involved in politics after leaving the army and joined a forerunner of the Nazi Party in 1919, becoming its leader in 1921. He was a **charismatic** leader who gave powerful and rousing speeches, blaming the Treaty of Versailles and the Jews for Germany's problems. His rallying cries to restore Germany's military might, create more jobs, and bring order amid the political and economic chaos helped to strengthen support for the Nazis, particularly among the young.

THE SA AND SS

Nazis in brown shirts called "Stormtroopers" (the SA) beat up opponents and attacked Jews. Another violent group, the SS, was formed in 1925 as Hitler's own guard. Hitler was eager to get the big industrial companies and the army on his side. These powerful figures were often criticized by the SA, so in 1934 Hitler had many SA leaders murdered. This was called the "Night of the Long Knives."

Ernst Röhm (center) was a founding member and commander of the SA. He was murdered during the "Night of the Long Knives."

FANNING THE FLAMES

Hitler became chancellor, or head of the German government, in 1933. Shortly afterward, the Reichstag, the German parliament building in Berlin, was set on fire. A Dutch communist was arrested for the attack. To this day historians disagree as to whether this was the work of one man, a wider communist plot, or whether it was all set up by the Nazis. Whatever the cause, the fire gave Hitler the excuse he needed to increase his powers.

Flames engulf the Reichstag parliament building during the fire of February 27, 1933.

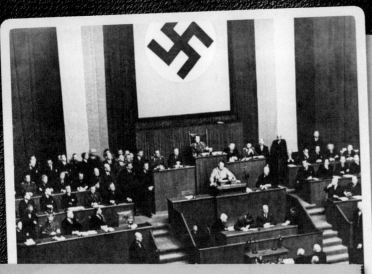

The passing of the Enabling Act in parliament. A large "swastika," a symbol of the Nazis, hangs on the wall.

ABSOLUTE POWER

On March 24, 1933, a special Enabling Act was passed in Germany. It gave Hitler the powers of a **dictator**—a ruler with absolute power. Communists and other political opponents, including elected members of the parliament, were rounded up and arrested. A secret police force, the much-feared Gestapo, was also founded. Then the persecution of the Jews began in earnest.

HITLER'S RALLIES

During the 1920s and 30s the Nazi party staged vast rallies at Nürnberg (Nuremberg) in Bavaria, Germany. The rallies commemorated those who died in World War I. There were also massive parades by the SA, the SS, and an organization for young Nazi followers called the Hitler Youth movement. Hundreds of thousands of voices roared their support for the *Führer* (the Leader), Adolf Hitler. In his speeches, Hitler ranted and raged against the Jews. In this photograph of a Nuremberg rally you can see Adolf Hitler (left) standing at the front with Ernst Röhm, commander of the SA (right).

"RACIAL SUPERIORITY"

THE BELIEF THAT HUMANS COULD BE DIVIDED INTO **RACES**, SOME OF WHICH WERE SUPERIOR TO OTHERS, WAS VERY COMMON IN EUROPE DURING THE 1800s AND 1900s. SUCH VIEWS WERE USED TO JUSTIFY SLAVERY AND EUROPEAN RULE IN OTHER LANDS.

Those in power believed that other races were not their equals, that they were stupid or lazy or criminal. Several scientists and scholars of the day thought this was likely to be true.

A MASTER RACE?

The word "Aryan" was first used to describe the speakers of Indo-European languages in Northern India, Iran, and in Southern and Western Europe. **Antisemitic** (anti-Jewish) campaigners picked up the term and claimed that Aryans were an ancient "master" race, of whom "Nordic" peoples such as the Germans were perfect examples. They believed that mixing with peoples such as the Jews had "contaminated" the Aryan race. The truth was that Europe, throughout history, had always seen a changing mixture of peoples, and that Europe's rich culture had in fact been strengthened by diversity.

22

This Nazi poster shows a German girl collecting money for youth hostels. Blond and blue-eyed, she was a perfect example of what they believed to be the Aryan "master race."

Young members of the Nazi security forces reading a copy of Mein Kampf *in 1939.*

MEIN KAMPF

"Purity" of race was the basis of a book that Adolf Hitler had started to write in jail in 1924. *Mein Kampf* (*My Struggle*, 1925) described the Jewish "peril." He claimed there was a Jewish conspiracy, or secret plan, to gain world leadership and that some political activists, such as communists and **socialists**, as well as big business, were all taking part in this international plot.

At the Hartheim Hospital, Austria, the Nazis went as far as killing handicapped people in so-called "mercy killings."

EUGENICS

Another popular theory in the 1900s was called **eugenics**. This was the idea that "better" human beings could be produced by breeding the cleverest, fittest, or strongest people. This view was widely respected at the time, but it was a dangerous idea. In Germany, France, the United Kingdom, and the USA some mental patients were sterilized so that they could not have children. The Nazis extended this policy to the physically disabled, deaf, and blind. In 1939, they began the so-called "mercy killings" of people with disabilities. The use of poison gas to kill people was first developed for mental patients in 1940.

NAZI PROPAGANDA

An illustration from an anti-Jewish educational picture book called *Don't Trust a Fox in a Green Meadow—or the Word of a Jew.* The words on the notice say, "Jews Not Wanted Here."

BOOKS AND POSTERS

Joseph Goebbels was the Nazi Minister of Propaganda beginning in 1933. **Propaganda** is a way of influencing and changing public opinion and political views. The Nazis used children's picture books, leaflets, posters, newspapers, cartoons, radio, and film to spread lies and racist hatred. Idealized "Aryans" were shown as young, fit, blond, and blue-eyed. Jews were portrayed as middle-aged, ugly, and grasping. Imaginary "Jewish" features such as hooked noses were ridiculed. Jews were even shown as vermin and lice, and accused of spreading disease and contaminating the purity of the "master race."

"The Eternal Jew" poster portrays a Jew as ugly, greedy, and grasping. He is shown next to a hammer and sickle—a symbol of communism.

The cover of Don't Trust a Fox in a Green Meadow —or the Word of a Jew. *This antisemitic picture book was widely read in German schools.*

In contrast, this poster shows a member of the Hitler Youth movement—he's young, healthy, and Aryan.

PERSECUTION

AFTER 1933, GERMANY'S PERSECUTION OF ITS JEWISH POPULATION BECAME EVER HARSHER. IN 1938, GERMANY ANNEXED (TOOK OVER) THE NEIGHBORING COUNTRY OF AUSTRIA, WHERE THE PERSECUTION OF THE JEWS ALSO TOOK HOLD.

The cruelty took many forms. Much of it was designed to humiliate and terrorize. Jews who made complaints against the Nazis were paraded around town with signs around their necks. In Austria's capital, Vienna, Jews were forced to kneel and scrub the city streets by hand. Any non-Jewish people who helped or made friends with Jews were punished as well.

A member of the Nazi SA stands outside a Jewish-owned store. The posters on the window are telling people to stop shopping at this store.

FORCED OUT OF WORK

Beginning in April 1933 the Nazis encouraged all Germans to avoid Jewish-owned shops. Jews were no longer allowed to own land, and starting in 1934 they were refused health insurance. In 1936-37 Jews were forced out of important jobs and government departments. In 1938 they were made to sell and close their businesses, and in 1939 they were ordered to hand over any gold and silver. The Nazis grew rich from the proceeds. Jews who left the country were not allowed to take any money or valuables with them.

LOSS OF CIVIL RIGHTS

At a Nuremberg convention in 1935, the Nazis introduced a law that deprived all Jews of German citizenship and banned marriage and sexual relations between Germans and Jews. Later, Jewish women were forced to add the "Jewish-sounding" name Sarah to their documents and men were forced to add the name Israel. Their passports were stamped with a large "J." Special courts were created that took away the right for Jews to appeal against a court verdict. By the end of 1941, Jews in Germany and Austria were forced to wear a yellow star that identified them as Jewish.

Members of the Hitler Youth burning books on a bonfire in Salzburg, Austria, 1938.

BURNING OF BOOKS

The Nazis also targeted the world of ideas. Bonfires were lit in cities and university towns all over Germany, and students and SA thugs threw books that were said to be "un-German" onto them. These included works by everyone the Nazis hated, including many Jewish authors. The writings of Heinrich Heine, a famous German writer, went up in the blaze. So too did the theories of the Nobel Prize–winning physicist Albert Einstein.

Jewish men are forced to scrub the streets of Vienna, Austria, in 1938.

"My grandfather Ernst owned a furniture factory in Darmstadt. In 1938 he was forced to sell it at a rock-bottom price to a non-Jewish businessman with Nazi party connections. He was later arrested by the Gestapo. They then reported that Ernst had committed suicide in his cell. It seemed more likely to the family that he had been murdered."

Michael Trier, grandson of a Jewish factory owner from Darmstadt, Germany

27

THE NIGHT OF BROKEN GLASS

On November 7, 1938, a Polish Jew, whose family had been persecuted by the Nazis, shot a German **diplomat** in Paris. During the night of November 9-10, 1938, the Nazis used this as an excuse to launch a pogrom, a deadly attack on Jews in towns throughout Germany and Austria. Rioters armed with hammers took to the streets, while the police stood by watching. Many thousands of Jewish businesses were destroyed. More than 1,000 synagogues were burnt to the ground and shop windows were smashed. So many splinters of glass lay on the pavements the next day that this event became known as *Kristallnacht* ("the night of broken glass"). Many Jews were murdered. Over 25,000 were imprisoned in **concentration camps** such as Dachau, where they were forced to do backbreaking physical work.

THE REFUGEES

AFTER 1933, THOUSANDS OF GERMAN JEWS DECIDED TO LEAVE GERMANY TO ESCAPE PERSECUTION.

Many of them migrated to other European countries, such as France—only to find themselves facing Nazi persecution all over again when Germany invaded France in 1940. Others reached safety in countries that were not invaded, such as Switzerland and Portugal. After *Kristallnacht* in 1938, many more Jews realized that the nightmare they were living through was not going to end anytime soon.

CLOSED DOORS

In July 1938, President Franklin D. Roosevelt called an international conference at Evian, France, to deal with the **refugee** crisis. Only one of the 32 countries taking part—the Dominican Republic—agreed to take any extra refugees beyond the agreed quota of 30,000. In May 1939, a German ship, the *St. Louis*, sailed across the Atlantic Ocean with 937 passengers, mostly refugees. They were refused permission to land in Cuba and the USA. In the United Kingdom and the USA, some parts of the press campaigned against allowing in any more German Jewish refugees.

This photograph shows Jewish refugees being sent back to the St. Louis, *having been refused entry to Cuba.*

These refugees from Vienna, Austria, were some of the lucky few who managed to escape the Nazis. Many of them never saw their relatives again.

Kindertransport *children from Germany arrive in London by train in February 1939.*

THE *KINDERTRANSPORT*

Between 1938 and 1940, Jewish, Christian, and **humanitarian** organizations persuaded the British government to allow in nearly 10,000 Jewish children without their parents. Desperate Jewish families sent their children off into an unknown future. The children of this *Kindertransport* ("children's transport program") traveled by train and ship, and were placed in foster homes and hostels around the United Kingdom, or traveled on to other countries. Many of the children's parents and relatives would later die during the Holocaust and never see their children again.

THE EXILES

The Jewish refugees who did manage to find a safe haven in the Americas, Asia, or unoccupied Europe were not always welcomed. Adults who had settled in the countries fighting Germany in World War II found that they were **interned** as "enemy aliens." In the United Kingdom, a change of policy eventually allowed adult Jews from Germany and Central Europe to join the armed forces and continue the fight against the Nazis. Some exiles, including famous writers, filmmakers, artists, and scientists, such as Albert Einstein, fled to the USA. In this way, Hitler's loss was America's gain.

Albert Einstein was a Nobel Prize-winning scientist who made important discoveries in the field of physics.

PART II: FROM WAR TO GENOCIDE

In March 1939, German troops marched into Czechoslovakia. In September, Germany invaded Poland. German tanks quickly swept across Europe in what they called *Blitzkrieg,* or "Lightning Warfare," taking the armies of the countries they invaded by surprise. This led to the start of World War II. As the war progressed, Adolf Hitler and the Nazis stepped up the persecution of Jews and other victims to another level of horror.

WAR RETURNS TO EUROPE

DURING WORLD WAR II (1939-1945), NAZI GERMANY SIDED WITH FASCIST ITALY AND JAPAN. THEY WERE JOINED BY ROMANIA, HUNGARY, AND BULGARIA. TOGETHER THEY WERE KNOWN AS THE AXIS POWERS. AS GERMAN TANKS INVADED OTHER COUNTRIES THEY WERE OPPOSED BY NATIONAL ARMIES BUT MADE FAST GAINS.

The Allies who continued the fight against Germany and the Axis powers included the United Kingdom and its **Commonwealth** and empire nations (such as Canada, Australia, and India), and also China. The communist **Soviet Union**, or USSR, joined the conflict when it was invaded by the Germans in 1941. It fought an epic war against Hitler across Eastern Europe. Beginning in December 1941, the Allies were joined by the powerful forces of the USA.

German tanks and motorcycles roll into Poland during the invasion of September 1939.

EUROPE IS OVERRUN

Germany seized control of Czechoslovakia in 1938-39, and in 1939 invaded Poland. France, Belgium, and the Netherlands fell to the Germans in 1940, as did Denmark and Norway. In April 1941, the Germans marched south into the Balkans, invading Yugoslavia and Greece. In June 1941, the Germans broke a peace agreement with the Soviet Union and ordered their troops eastwards into the Baltic states. Their aim was to take over the fertile farmlands of the east for German settlement. They claimed that the "master race" deserved more "space to live," in one nation known as the German Reich.

IRELAND

UNITED KINGDOM

NETHER LANDS

BELGIUM

FRANCE

SWITZE LAND

VICHY FRANCE

PORTUGAL

SPAIN

This map shows Europe at the height of Nazi expansion in 1942.

Allies

Neutral

Germany or German occupied

Germany's allies or areas occupied by Germany's allies

OCCUPIED PEOPLES

In the lands the Germans invaded they were often supported by local sympathizers or collaborators. In some occupied countries the Nazis set up governments that were prepared to cooperate with them, such as the "French State" government based at Vichy, in southern France. However, the Nazis were also attacked by bands of **resistance fighters**, or **partisans**. Many people who had escaped the Nazi invasion formed their own fighting forces based overseas, such as the Free French, based in London. Within Germany and the occupied countries, there were at least 16 plots to assassinate Adolf Hitler, but none succeeded.

French resistance fighters are rounded up by forces from the pro-Nazi Vichy government.

Women, such as these Italian partisans, played a vital role in the resistance forces.

Map labels
NORWAY
FINLAND
SWEDEN
SOVIET UNION
DENMARK
REICHS KOMMISSARIAT OSTLAND (former Estonia, Latvia, and Lithuania)
GERMAN REICH
(former Poland)
GENERAL GOVERNMENT
REICHS KOMMISSARIAT UKRAINE
BOHEMIA & MORAVIA (former Czechoslovakia)
SLOVAKIA
(former Austria)
HUNGARY
CROATIA
ROMANIA
(former Yugoslavia)
SERBIA
ITALY
MONTE-NEGRO
BULGARIA
ALBANIA
GREECE
TURKEY
CYPRUS

THE CENTER OF THE STORM

Before the Holocaust, Germany had a Jewish population of about 565,000. Poland had Europe's biggest Jewish population, at 3,000,000. In the European region of the Soviet Union, there were 2,525,000 Jews. Many Jews also lived in Greece, Bulgaria, Hungary, Romania, Czechoslovakia, the Netherlands, and France. As the war raged across Europe, these communities were at the center of the storm.

GHETTOS AND CAMPS

THE WORD "TERRORIST" IS USED TO DESCRIBE NATIONS AND INDIVIDUALS WHO USE FEAR AND VIOLENCE TO TRY TO BRING ABOUT POLITICAL CHANGE. During World War II, the Nazis enforced terrorist rule in Germany and in occupied Europe by imprisonment, torture, forced labor, internment in ghettos and camps, and mass murder. The German Special Courts in Poland could pass the death sentence for almost any "offense."

THE GHETTOS

The Germans created over 1,000 ghettos in Central and Eastern Europe in order to control the Jewish population. These were restricted areas in cities where Jews were forced to live. Some Jews were recruited for the Jewish police force in the ghettos. Many of the ghettos in Poland were walled in and surrounded by barbed wire. People were packed into the overcrowded houses without enough food or proper **sanitation.** Many of the inhabitants of the ghettos were later transported to concentration camps, where a great number died.

Children on the streets of the Warsaw ghetto in Poland, 1941.

THE CAMPS

The first Nazi concentration camp was Dachau, built in Germany in 1933. It was the model for many more. During World War II there may have been thousands of camps and subcamps in Germany and in the occupied countries. Some were internment or prison camps. Some were forced labor camps, or camps where people were placed after being deported from their homes. At all of these camps, starvation and death were common. In 1942, the Germans began to build **extermination camps** with one purpose only—mass murder. Most of these camps were in occupied Poland, and 90 percent of the victims were Jews.

The gate at the Dachau forced labor camp displayed the sinister words "Arbeit Macht Frei"—"Work Brings Freedom."

DEATH SQUADS

During World War II the Nazis set up *Einsatzgruppen* ("task forces") to work alongside police units and the armed forces as death squads. By the end of the war they had murdered about 1.5 million people, over half of them Jews. In September 1941, they shot dead 33,711 Jews in just two days at the Babi Yar ravine, Kiev, the Ukraine. Tens of thousands of Roma, Soviet prisoners of war, and political opponents were also shot at this site during the occupation. Romanian and German troops also carried out massacres of over 100,000 Jews around Odessa, in the Ukraine, during the war.

The Einsatzgruppen *"death squads" killed thousands of people in the Ukraine.*

The wild grasses rustle over Babi Yar.
The trees look ominous, like judges.
Here all things scream silently, and, baring my head,
Slowly I feel myself turning gray.

From the poem "Babi Yar" by
Yevgeny Yevtushenko, 1961

THE WARSAW GHETTO

This famous photograph shows SS guards rounding up Jews in the Warsaw ghetto in Poland to be transported to concentration camps. The Warsaw ghetto was the largest Jewish ghetto in Nazi-occupied Europe, with some 450,000 Jews living in unbearable, overcrowded conditions. Severe food rationing caused many to die of starvation. In April 1943, some of the Jews resisted the Germans in a bitter struggle known as the Warsaw Ghetto Uprising. However, very few survived.

39

ANNE FRANK'S DIARY

Otto Frank and his wife, Edith, were Jews from Frankfurt-am-Main, in Germany. They had two daughters, Margot and Annelies, or "Anne." In 1933, they moved to Amsterdam, in the Netherlands, to start a new life. When the Germans invaded the Netherlands in 1940, they again faced Nazi persecution. By 1942, things had become so bad that the family hid in secret rooms in Otto's workplace, where they were helped by some of his colleagues. Later they were joined by others who were in hiding.

The 13-year-old Anne kept a record of day-to-day life in her diary, over two years. It describes what life was like in the cramped conditions. In 1944, the German police were tipped off to the family's hiding place by an informer. The Franks were arrested and sent to Auschwitz concentration camp, in Poland. Otto survived, but Edith died of starvation. Anne and Margot were transported to the camp at Bergen-Belsen, where they died of **typhus** in 1945. After the war, Anne's diary was given to Otto, and it was published in 1947.

Anne Frank's original red check diary. The diary was later translated into over 60 languages.

Ukrainian Jewish families hid in caves in the forest.

HIDDEN CAVES

When the Germans invaded the Soviet Union, they came to a Ukrainian town called Korolówka. The Jews living there were killed, or sent off to the Borszczów ghetto or to the extermination camp at Belzec. But Esther and Zaida Stermer and their six children, as well as several other families, took to the forest and hid in two dark underground caves for almost two years. By night they foraged for food. They were finally liberated by Soviet troops in April 1944.

The Stermer children and relatives in 2012.

"I don't think of all the misery, but of the beauty that still remains."

Anne Frank, "The Diary of a Young Girl" (1947)

Warsaw Zoo, Poland, in 1938.

AT THE ZOO

Moshe Tirosh used to be called Mieczyslaw Kenigswein. He was a little Jewish boy who lived in Warsaw, Poland. His family escaped from the ghetto and hid in the city. One night his father, Samuel, a carpenter, took his family to the city zoo. This was no normal visit, for it was dark and rainy, and they had to get past German patrols. The Polish director of the zoo, Jan Zabinski, and his wife, Antonina, took Moshe's family in. He offered Jews refuge in the basement and in the underground tunnels between the animal cages. Jan also stored weapons there. During the war about 300 Jewish lives were saved by a trip to the zoo.

The entrance to the secret rooms in Otto Frank's former workplace lay behind a big bookcase.

JEWISH RESISTANCE

ONCE THE NAZIS HAD TOTAL POWER IN GERMANY AND IN OCCUPIED EUROPE, IT WAS VERY HARD FOR ANY CIVILIANS TO RESIST THEM. THOSE WHO TRIED WERE IMMEDIATELY SENT TO PRISON OR CAMPS, WHERE THEY WERE TORTURED OR KILLED.

For Jews who had been stripped of their citizenship it was even harder. They were isolated and had nowhere to hide. The bravest were often the first to die. Nevertheless, some Jewish individuals and groups did take up arms against the Nazis.

Though vastly outnumbered by the Nazis, Jewish resistance fighters in the Warsaw ghetto fought back for three weeks.

Resistance fighters in the Warsaw ghetto are rounded up by the German military.

GHETTO UPRISINGS

There were about 100 uprisings by Jews trapped in the ghettos of Poland and Eastern Europe. When the Germans ordered **deportation** to extermination camps such as Treblinka, the younger and fitter Jews attacked the guards with weapons they had smuggled in. The fiercest uprising was in the Warsaw ghetto, in 1943. The Jewish resistance hid families and built defensive bunkers, fighting the Germans with pistols and explosives. The rebels put up a hard fight but were eventually overcome and forced to surrender.

42

BREAKING OUT

Even in the harshest camps, such as Treblinka, Auschwitz, and Sobibor, there was Jewish resistance. Desperate prisoners would steal pickaxes or guns and set fire to the camp or try to break through the wire. Some succeeded in joining up with local partisans, although some of these partisan groups in Poland and Eastern Europe were antisemitic themselves. Many of the rebels died in minefields outside the camps or were recaptured and shot.

Buildings were set on fire during the prisoner uprising in Treblinka in 1943.

Adriana Scriabina was a founder of the Armée Juive. *She was killed by Nazi collaborators in 1944.*

FIGHTING IN FRANCE

Jewish resistance groups also organized themselves in occupied France and in Vichy France. An *Armée Juive* (Jewish Army) was founded in France, to help Jews escape across the border to Spain (which was neutral during the war) and also to fight the Germans. *Solidarité*, a Jewish communist group, attacked the Germans in Paris. Many Jews also joined the wider French resistance movement. Jewish resistance groups lacked the weapons and resources to dent the Nazis' war machine, but their courage was a powerful symbol to others.

43

THE "FINAL SOLUTION"

The Nazis used harmless-sounding language to mask their most extreme policies. They talked of the "Final Solution." However, they were not talking of an end to the war, but a plan to murder the entire Jewish population of Europe. On January 20 ,1942, a senior SS officer named Reinhard Heydrich called a conference at a grand villa at Wannsee, a lakeside suburb of Berlin. The *Einsatzgruppen* death squads were already shooting and hanging thousands of Jews in Eastern Europe. Now the proposal was for the SS to take control of the killings and organize a Europe-wide program of mass murder. Trains, such as the one in this photograph, would bring Jews from cities all over occupied Europe to extermination camps.

DEPORTATION

THE REMOVAL OF PEOPLE FROM A COUNTRY IS CALLED "DEPORTATION." UNDER NAZI RULE IT OFTEN STARTED WITH A KNOCK ON THE DOOR, AN ARREST AT THE POLICE STATION, AND THEN A JOURNEY TO A **TRANSIT CAMP.**
Trains then took prisoners onward across Europe, to labor and extermination camps. The "Final Solution" was organized with cold-hearted efficiency and no regard for humanity.

This map shows the locations of major Nazi concentration and extermination camps in Europe.

◇ Transit Camp

● Concentration camp

☐ Extermination camp

■ Allied territory

■ German occupied territory

■ Neutral territory

■ Territory occupied by Germany's allies

UNITED KINGDOM

Breendonk

Drancy ◇

FRANCE

Natzweiler

VICHY FRANCE

Thousands of Jews and other prisoners were rounded up at the Winter Stadium before being transported to Auschwitz-Birkenau.

THE WINTER STADIUM, PARIS

In the summer of 1942, the Nazis ordered French police—aided by French fascists—to round up any Jews in the region who were from Germany, Central, or Eastern Europe. In Paris, about 8,000 of those arrested were packed into the city's indoor cycling track, the Winter Stadium. The prisoners had no sanitation, and little food or water. Anyone who tried to escape was shot. They suffered there for five days before being taken to camps in France and then on to be murdered in Poland. Within three months of the stadium roundup, 38,000 Jews had been deported from France to Auschwitz.

CATTLE TRUCKS

The train journeys to the camps were terrifying. Men, women, and small children were pushed by guards into overcrowded cattle trucks, which were then locked. They had very little to eat or drink and no sanitation. They were bitterly cold in winter and overcome with heat in summer. There were no windows, just wooden slats. The journeys often took several days, as the trains stopped to take on more prisoners.

Hungarian Jews are forced to line up as they disembark from the trains at Auschwitz.

Bergen-Belsen

Ravensbruck

Sachsenhausen

ora-Mittelbau

Chelmno

GERMAN REICH

Treblinka

Buchenwald

Gross-Rosen

Majdanek

Sobibor

Flossenbürg

Theresienstadt

Auschwitz

Belzec

Terezín

Plaszow

Dachau

SLOVAKIA

Mauthausen

HUNGARY

TZERLAND

RAILWAY COMPANIES

Many national rail companies collaborated with the Nazis to bring about the "Final Solution." The Germans took over Polish National Railways when they invaded, and imprisoned or shot the management. Polish rail workers who tried to stop the trains by **sabotage** were hanged alongside the tracks as a grim warning to others.

ITALY

CROATIA

47

END OF THE LINE

Several camps were set up at Auschwitz during World War II. Auschwitz II–Birkenau was a concentration camp and an extermination camp. The first trains arrived there in March 1942. From spring 1944 the railway track went right into the camp itself. As the doors of the wagons were opened, the prisoners were dazzled by the first light they had seen in days. They stumbled or were pulled out. Men and women were divided. Their belongings were taken from them and they were made to line up for examination. Most were selected for instant death. About one in five were selected for forced labor. Most of these would also later die, from starvation, exhaustion, or disease.

49

PRISONERS AND SYMBOLS

THE NAZIS USED A COLOR-CODING SYSTEM TO ORGANIZE INMATES IN CONCENTRATION CAMPS. JEWS HAD TO WEAR YELLOW STARS. ROMA AND SINTI VICTIMS WORE A BROWN TRIANGLE. CRIMINALS WORE A GREEN TRIANGLE. Political prisoners were identified by a red triangle, and homosexual prisoners by a pink one. The Nazis also targeted many Christian and non-Christian groups. **Jehovah's Witnesses**, who refused to fight, and some **pacifists**, were identified by a purple or black triangle.

This table shows some of the identification badges that the Nazis had sewn onto the clothes of their prisoners.

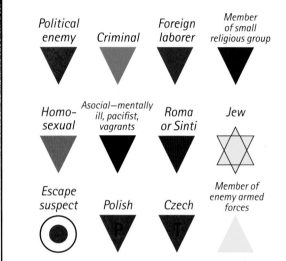

Political enemy	Criminal	Foreign laborer	Member of small religious group
▼	▼	▼	▼
Homo-sexual	Asocial—mentally ill, pacifist, vagrants	Roma or Sinti	Jew
▼	▼	▼	✡
Escape suspect	Polish	Czech	Member of enemy armed forces
◉	▼P	▼T	△

The tattooed prisoner number of Leon Greenman, who was imprisoned in six different concentration camps during the war.

TATTOOS AND NUMBERS

In many camps, prisoners were also identified by serial numbers printed on their jackets. At Auschwitz from 1941 on, numbers were tattooed onto the skin of prisoners, to help record their death or to identify them if they tried to escape. To those who survived the camps, these tattoos remained a lifetime reminder of their ordeal and their courage.

SLAVS AND POWs

The Nazis murdered many millions of Slavs, whom they believed to be of an inferior race. These included Poles, Czechs, Ukrainians, and Serbs. Over three million Soviet prisoners of war (POWs) were killed in the death camps, even though the Geneva Convention of 1929 (an international agreement) was supposed to protect all POWs. Some Soviet soldiers were the first camp victims to be killed with a deadly gas called Zyklon B. Communists and other political opponents of the Nazis were murdered, too.

A group of Roma at Belzec camp in 1942. Belzec was the first camp to have gas chambers built for the purpose of killing.

ROMA AND SINTI

These peoples were often known in English as "Gypsies" (from "Egyptians"). In fact they had originally come from northern India, migrating westward in the early medieval era. Because they were traveling peoples who kept their own customs, they were often persecuted. The Nazis decided they were a "criminal" race—even when they had committed no crime. They were deported, forced into slave labor, shot in mass killings by death squads, or murdered in camps such as Auschwitz and Treblinka. Between 200,000 and 600,000 may have been killed.

A monument in Tel Aviv, Israel, dedicated to the gay and lesbian victims of the Holocaust. It was opened in 2014.

GAY VICTIMS OF THE NAZIS

During the 1920s, gay and lesbian cafés, bars, and meeting places had been popular in Berlin and in many other German cities. But under Nazi rule, homosexual men were sent to mental hospitals, prisons, or concentration camps. They were experimented on by doctors and brutally bullied by the guards. Many were killed through starvation and hard labor.

51

Soviet soldiers being rounded up by the Nazis. Over 3 million Soviet POWs were murdered in Nazi camps.

LIFE IN THE CAMPS

THE SS GUARDS AND COMMANDANTS WHO RAN THE CONCENTRATION CAMPS DID THEIR BEST TO **"DEHUMANIZE"** AND STAMP OUT THE INDIVIDUALITY OF EVERY PRISONER. To the Nazi regime the prisoners were not people, they were just a mass of bodies that needed to be contained and kept apart from the "acceptable" communities of Germans. The daily routines in the camps were rigid and unbending, carefully designed to break the human spirit and wear down any last traces of resistance.

Inmates had their clothes taken away and often wore striped uniforms like these.

Prisoners slept in wooden bunk beds on straw or a thin blanket.

WAKING AND WASHING

A camp prisoner's day began with an early-morning wake-up call, followed by a wash in dirty water. The toilets in the barracks were filthy and crowded: Often, 2,000 or so inmates would have to share a wooden board that had just 100 holes in it. There was no soap, no privacy, and very few chances for the prisoners to change out of filthy or torn clothing. Weeks or months would go by before any new garments were offered.

THE ROLL CALL

Washing was followed by the *Appell*, the daily roll call. The prisoners were forced to stand completely still, in rows. This sometimes lasted for hours and hours, even if the weather was extremely bad. The guards used this time to count the prisoners and read out long lists of instructions for the day or orders for individual inmates. They also taunted the prisoners, shouting into their faces or suddenly beating one of them to the ground, making the others freeze with fear. Sometimes the guards would decide to torture them further—by doing the count all over again.

Guards oversee a roll call at the Dachau concentration camp in Germany.

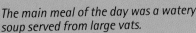

The main meal of the day was a watery soup served from large vats.

> "We had only one blanket, but we covered ourselves with our coats. We were together and it was a great help."
>
> Helga Weiss, a Holocaust survivor from Prague

MEAL TIMES

Food in a concentration camp was deliberately scarce. The meals were designed to keep the prisoners alive, but they didn't provide enough energy for the hard labor that some of the inmates had to do. For breakfast or lunch, all they got was some watery soup, a piece of bread, and a hot drink. In the evenings, the inmates were lucky if they got some extra bread, plus some marmalade, sausage, or cheese. It is no surprise, then, that so many thousands starved or died from illnesses brought on by the lack of food.

53

DEATH CAMPS

SOME CAMPS, SUCH AS CHELMNO, TREBLINKA, BELZEC, AND SOBIBOR WERE BUILT PURELY AS EXTERMINATION CAMPS. OTHER DEATH CAMPS, SUCH AS AUSCHWITZ-BIRKENAU, WERE ALSO CENTERS FOR SLAVE LABOR. The "Final Solution" was ordered by the Nazi leadership, but it was carried out by "ordinary" people—by factory owners, railway officials, doctors, soldiers, guards, clerks, secretaries, and other workers.

"The discussion covered killing, eliminating and annihilation."

Adolf Eichmann, 1961. He describes what was discussed at the Nazi Wannsee Conference in 1942, when the "Final Solution" was put into operation.

PRISONERS

MAIN G

54

A CRUEL DECEPTION

Prisoners who were selected to be killed on arrival at a death camp were often tricked into believing that they had arrived at a transit camp or a labor camp. They were lined up and ordered to strip. Then they were led into what appeared to be a shower block, actually a gas chamber, with tiled walls. Some who realized the truth would panic. They were led away and shot. Others tried to comfort their fellow victims while the doors were locked behind them.

Women and children are divided up after arrival at Auschwitz. Some would be sent straight to the gas chambers.

THE GAS CHAMBERS

The Nazis' early experiments with poison gas used vans equipped as mobile killing units. Later, large permanent gas chambers were built at the death camps. Carbon monoxide gas was replaced in 1942 by a deadly chemical called hydrogen cyanide, which was traded under the name Zyklon B. SS guards dropped pellets into the gas chambers. It could take 20 minutes for victims to die.

ZYKLON B

GIFTGAS!

Gasapparat! Kühl und trocken lagern! Vor Sonne und offener Flamme schützen! Nur durch geübtes Personal zu öffnen und zu verwenden!

CYANGEHALT: 200 g

KALIWERKE A. G., KOLIN.

A container of the poisonous Zyklon B gas that was used by the Nazis to kill prisoners.

PRISONERS

PRISONERS

UNDRESSING ROOM

CREMATORIUM II

GAS CHAMBER

CREMATORIUM

ENGINE ROOM

An aerial photograph of Auschwitz-Birkenau death camp taken by a US military plane in 1944.

BOX

UNDRESSING ROOM

GA

ASHES AND DUST

Other prisoners were forced to remove the dead bodies. Sometimes these included the remains of their friends and relatives. The bodies were stripped of any rings or jewelry. Even gold fillings were taken from the teeth. The bodies were then burnt, either on open-air fires, or, as at Auschwitz, in **crematoria**. The tall, smoking chimneys from these ovens towered over the camp. The ashes were buried or scattered.

Prisoners had all their personal belongings, including eyeglasses, taken away.

55

CHILD VICTIMS

About 1,500,000 children, including babies, died during the Holocaust. Over a million of them were Jewish, while tens of thousands were Roma and Sinti. Some were killed by death squads in Eastern Europe; others died of diseases, infections, or starvation during transit, in ghettos, or at the extermination camps. A few of them escaped. This photograph shows children peering out from the fences at Auschwitz-Birkenau camp in 1945.

VOICES OF THE YOUNG

THE NAZIS CARED LITTLE ABOUT THE SUFFERING OF CHILDREN FROM "UNWANTED" GROUPS SINCE THEY SAW IT AS PART OF THE "RACIAL STRUGGLE" TO PREVENT THE EXPANSION OF A "DANGEROUS" POPULATION. The very young and weak were most at risk of losing their lives, while older, stronger children were sometimes used as slave labor. Families were split up and never saw each other again.

Children who were selected to live had their heads shaved, were given a striped uniform and a number, and were then photographed.

A CRUEL FATE

Because children under 14 were considered too young to be used as forced labor, they were often the first to be killed in mass shootings or deported to the death camps and selected for the gas chambers soon after arrival. Others were selected for cruel medical experiments by SS doctors such as Dr. Josef Mengele. Mengele was particularly interested in carrying out experiments on twins. Many of his victims died during the experimental procedures.

A memorial to Janusz Korczak and his orphans in Jerusalem.

WORDS AND PICTURES

Petr Ginz was a part-Jewish boy from Prague, Czechoslovakia. He was transported to Theresienstadt concentration camp in October 1942. The Nazis intended this camp to be for Jewish artists, writers, scientists, and musicians, and it had a rich cultural life. Petr was a talented writer and illustrator. At the camp he edited the magazine *Vedem*, which means "We Lead." It included articles and illustrations created by him. He also wrote a diary detailing day-to-day events before and during his time at the camp. Petr was transported to Auschwitz in 1944, where he was gassed at the age of 16. "The Diary of Petr Ginz" was published in 2007.

Petr Ginz as a boy in Prague before the war.

Petr Ginz's watercolor-and-ink illustration of the living quarters at Theresienstadt.

FOR THE ORPHANS

Janusz Korczak was a Polish-Jewish doctor, educator, and writer who ran an orphanage in the Warsaw ghetto. During the Holocaust, many children's parents died from disease or starvation, and Korczak and his colleagues offered them shelter. When the Nazis deported the children to Treblinka, Korczak refused an offer of help from Polish friends and accompanied the children to the camp so they would not be alone. He died at Treblinka with the children.

ESCAPE ATTEMPTS

MASS ESCAPE FROM SOBIBOR

Jewish prisoners led a successful mass escape from Sobibor extermination camp in occupied Poland in October 1943. The camp's resistance had been planning the escape since the summer of 1943. In September 1943 some Soviet prisoners of war arrived at the camp and helped with the escape plans. On the night of October 14, the camp's resistance managed to overcome eleven SS officers and camp guards and cut the camp's phone lines. They were then able to break the camp's barbed wire and run into the surrounding forest. About 300 prisoners escaped that night but most were killed by mines surrounding the camp or by the Nazis who later rounded them up. However, about 58 are thought to have survived. The Nazis closed the camp at the end of 1943.

The story of the breakout from Sobibor was made into a film, Escape from Sobibor, *in 1987.*

The escapees managed to drive through the main gate of Auschwitz I.

A photograph of Kazimierz Piechowski as an inmate of Auschwitz.

THE BREAKOUT

Very few people escaped from Auschwitz and lived. One of the bravest and most daring escapes was organized in 1942 by a Polish man named Kazimierz Piechowski. He was a political prisoner who was forced to carry away dead bodies executed by the firing squads. He joined up with two other Poles, one of them a priest, and a Ukrainian car mechanic named Eugeniusz Bendera. They stole SS uniforms and a staff car. Then, they fooled the guards at the gate and made a getaway over forest tracks. Piechowski went on to join the partisans in their fight against the Nazis.

Piechowski and his fellow prisoners escaped in a Steyr car similar to this one.

Jews were transported to Chelmno, in Poland, in overcrowded trucks. Many were then sent to the gas vans.

THE WORD GETS OUT

Many Jews could not believe the rumors they heard about the death camps. Hardly anyone who went in came out to tell the truth to the outside world. In January 1942, a Polish Jew named Szlama ber Winer (also known as Yaakov Grojanowski) saw his own family killed in the gas vans in the extermination camp at Chelmno, Poland. He escaped from a work gang and made his way to the Warsaw ghetto. There, he reported the mass murders to the Jewish leaders, who told the Polish resistance movement what was going on behind the barbed wire. Winer was later captured and gassed at the Belzec death camp.

61

HEROES OF HUMANITY

CHEATING THE NAZIS

Oskar Schindler was a German factory owner from Moravia (now in the Czech Republic). He was also a spy for the German government and joined the Nazi party in 1939. In that year he bought a factory that made enamel pots and pans in Kraków, Poland. It had previously been owned by Jews. Many of Schindler's workers were Jews from the Kraków ghetto.

At first Schindler was only interested in his factory's profits, but he became horrified by the treatment of the Jews. With his powerful connections, he was able to protect his workers, even after they were deported to the Plaszow camp. Schindler managed to persuade the Nazis to let him build a subcamp outside the main Plaszow camp to house factory workers. He had to pay more and more in bribes to keep them safe. In the end he moved his factory to Moravia. He outsmarted the Nazis and probably saved over 1,200 Jewish lives.

Schindler's former factory in Kraków, Poland, is now a museum.

> "I had to help them. There was no choice."
>
> Oskar Schindler in 1964

Oskar Schindler, 1908–1974.

SCHINDLER'S LIST

The 1993 film Schindler's List told the story of Schindler and his protection of Jewish workers. It was directed by Steven Spielberg and won many awards.

Nicholas Winton with one of the children he rescued in 1939.

TRAINS TO FREEDOM

Nicholas Winton was from London and of German Jewish descent. From 1938 to1939 he organized the rescue of 669 children, most of them Jewish, from German-occupied Czechoslovakia. They traveled by train through four countries, and Winton had to battle to get permission from the authorities. He and his mother found foster homes and hostels for the refugees in the UK. He died on July 1, 2015, at the age of 106.

A photograph of Aristides de Sousa Mendes in 1940.

AN ESCAPE ROUTE

Eduardo Propper de Callejón was a Spanish diplomat who worked in Bordeaux, France, from 1940 to 1944. Also in Bordeaux at the time was a Portuguese **consul** named Aristides de Sousa Mendes. Without having the permission of Spain's foreign minister, the two officials issued passports and visas to Jews fleeing the Nazis. The precious papers allowed Jews to cross neutral Spain and enter Portugal. From there many took ships to the USA. Over 30,000 lives may have been saved in this way.

One of the visas issued to refugees by Aristides de Sousa Mendes.

PART III: FREEDOM AND REMEMBRANCE

The Holocaust lasted until World War II came to an end in Europe, on May 7–8, 1945. With the peace came joy and freedom, but also chaos, exhaustion, and a wider realization of the horrors that had taken place. The cities of Europe lay in ruins. **Displaced persons** searched desperately for their families. Many tried to build new lives for themselves, often in new lands.

Inmates celebrate at Dachau concentration camp after liberation by American troops in 1945.

AN END TO THE WAR

WORLD WAR II HAD SPREAD ACROSS THE WORLD, FROM NORTH AFRICA TO SINGAPORE, FROM THE ARCTIC OCEAN TO THE ISLANDS OF THE PACIFIC. WHOLE CITIES WERE BOMBED TO DESTRUCTION.

In late 1942, the tide of war at last began to turn against Adolf Hitler and the Nazis in Europe. In February 1943, the German 6th Army was destroyed by Soviet troops at Stalingrad. In July 1943, Allied troops invaded Italy to begin the liberation of Western Europe from the Nazis.

FROM WEST AND EAST

On June 6, 1944 (code-named "D-Day"), US, Canadian, British, and other Allied troops landed in Normandy, in occupied France, beginning an advance into Northwestern Europe. On March 22,1945, the US 3rd Army crossed the Rhine River in Germany. On April 25, as US troops advanced through Germany, they met up with Soviet troops at the Elbe River. During their advance from the east, the Russians had discovered the remains of the Nazi extermination camps. British and Canadian troops also encountered concentration camps as they came from the west. They reported what they found to the world.

A British soldier talks to an inmate of Belgen-Belsen during the liberation of the camp by the Allies.

66

The last official photo of Adolf Hitler shows him congratulating a member of the Hitler Youth in Berlin shortly before his death in April 1945.

THE DEATH OF HITLER

Since January 1945, Adolf Hitler and his partner, Eva Braun, had taken refuge in a concrete bomb shelter, or bunker, in Berlin, Germany's capital. By April many German troops were being defeated and captured by the Allies. The defense of Berlin was left to young boys and old men as the city was surrounded by the Soviet troops. Realizing that he was defeated, on April 30, 1945, Hitler shot himself, while Eva Braun, whom he had married the previous day, poisoned herself with a cyanide pill.

SURRENDER

On May 7, 1945, the Germans surrendered to the western Allies in Reims, France. The next day they surrendered to the Soviet Union in Berlin. The war in the Pacific continued until August, when the USA dropped **atomic bombs** on the Japanese cities of Hiroshima and Nagasaki, killing between 129,000 and 246,000 people. Japan announced its surrender on August 15 and World War II ended officially on September 2, 1945.

Alfred Jodl (center), Chief of the Operations Staff of the German armed forces, signs the unconditional surrender in Reims, France.

US troops wade ashore onto the beaches during the Allied invasion of Normandy, France, in 1944.

The end of the war in Europe became newspaper headlines by the evening of May 7, 1945.

BROKEN BERLIN

In the last months of the war, Germany and its capital, Berlin, were reduced to ruins. Bombing by the Western Allies and the Soviet assault on Berlin had smashed the city into piles of rubble. Once the war was over, Germany and Berlin itself were divided into different regions that were governed by the USA, the United Kingdom, France, and the Soviet Union. The tension between these Western countries and the Soviet Union soon led to the Cold War, a long period of hostility between the former Allies. Beginning in 1949, Germany was divided into two separate states, **capitalist** in the West and communist in the East. The country was finally unified in 1990.

THE CAMPS EXPOSED

THE REST OF THE WORLD HAD SOME IDEA OF THE EXTENT OF THE NAZIS' CRIMES AS THE WAR PROGRESSED. HOWEVER, FEW WERE PREPARED FOR THE HORRORS REVEALED AS ADVANCING ALLIED TROOPS LIBERATED THE CAMPS IN THE FINAL MONTHS OF THE WAR.

Soldiers, doctors, and nurses witnessed the effects of the Holocaust firsthand. They saw thousands of the dead and dying piled up in the yards. They saw starving people with shaved heads and staring eyes, who were little more than skin and bones. These were images that none of them would ever forget, as long as they lived.

INTO THE DEATH CAMPS

As the Soviet forces drew near, SS guards in the camps tried to destroy traces of their crimes. Many prisoners were killed or led away on so-called death marches to other camps. Thousands of them died of exhaustion or illness, or were executed on the way. Soviet troops now entered the big extermination camps of Majdanek and Auschwitz, where thousands had already been removed to other locations. They also liberated camps such as Stutthof, Sachsenhausen, and Ravensbrück, a women's concentration camp.

70

Prisoners from Dachau are marched through a German town on one of the so-called "death marches." Many perished due to starvation or illness.

A doctor from the Soviet army helps survivors from the newly liberated Auschwitz concentration camp in January 1945.

THE ROAD TO DACHAU

In April 1945, US troops discovered the slave labor camps of Ohrdruf and Dora-Mittelbau, where prisoners worked on Nazi V-2 long-range missiles. They freed 20,000 people from the Buchenwald concentration camp, near Weimar, and intercepted a death march from Flossenbürg to Dachau, where many prisoners were sick or dying.

Former prisoners of Mauthausen and Buchenwald are transported home on trucks after they have been freed.

The Allied troops who liberated the camps discovered inmates who were too weak to move and close to death.

THE HORRORS OF BELSEN

British and Canadian troops liberated camps to the north. Shocking scenes awaited them at Bergen-Belsen. This was a concentration and transit camp, not an extermination camp. However, at the end of the war, it had taken in thousands of extra prisoners from Auschwitz and other camps. Typhus was killing many of the prisoners. The troops found 10,000 naked dead bodies and 50,000 people in a state of extreme starvation, scarcely able to move. Even after medical care had arrived, 14,000 more died.

71

THE END OF THE CAMPS

Bergen-Belsen was a serious threat to public health. Once the concentration camp had been cleared by Allied troops, it was razed to the ground, using flame-throwers and tanks, shown in this photograph taken on May 21, 1945. Many other camps were destroyed for the same reason—to prevent the spread of diseases, such as typhus. Other camps such as Buchenwald were preserved to remind people of what had happened. Auschwitz became the most famous of these. In 1946, it was recognized as a state memorial to the victims of the Nazis, and in 1955 it was reopened as a museum. It is a place of pilgrimage for Holocaust survivors and for descendants of the victims.

73

BROUGHT TO JUSTICE

IN JANUARY 1946, THE ALLIES INTRODUCED A **DE-NAZIFICATION** PROGRAM IN GERMANY AND AUSTRIA. THROUGH THIS PROGRAM, THEY MADE CHANGES TO THE LAW AND TO EDUCATION, BANNED NAZI ORGANIZATIONS, AND REMOVED SYMBOLS OF NAZI POWER, SUCH AS THE SWASTIKA.

Many leading Nazis followed Adolf Hitler's example and committed suicide rather than face justice. Joseph Goebbels, one of the chief supporters of the Holocaust, took poison with his wife and their six children. The SS leader Heinrich Himmler, who was the main director of the Holocaust, killed himself in prison.

THE NUREMBERG TRIALS

From 1945 to 1946, leading Nazis were put on trial in Nuremberg, once the scene of huge pro-Nazi rallies. The trials were a collaborative effort of the Soviet Union, the USA, the United Kingdom, and France. Six organizations and 23 Nazi leaders were charged. Only 3 were found not guilty. Of the others, 12 were sentenced to death and the rest were imprisoned. Hermann Goering, former commander of the German air force, killed himself in his prison cell. From 1946 to 1949, US military trials at Nuremberg also tried doctors, lawyers, industrialists, army officers, and SS officers from the camps.

ESCAPE TO SOUTH AMERICA

Some Nazi criminals escaped to South America. Walter Rauff, the SS officer who invented the mobile gas chamber, lived in Chile and never faced trial. Josef Mengele, the doctor who carried out medical experiments on prisoners at Auschwitz, lived secretly in Argentina, Paraguay, and Brazil. Some ex-Nazis were protected by South American dictators and others were protected by European police officers who had themselves collaborated with the Nazis.

Josef Mengele (second from left) escaped to Brazil and evaded capture for the rest of his life. He died in 1979.

> "... a soldier's obligation to obey orders. That's the code I've lived by all my life."

Alfred Jodl, Chief of Operations, German High Command, at the Nuremberg War Trials, 1946

Nazi defendants at the Nuremberg Trials, including Hermann Goering (standing far left with headphones), commander of the German air force.

DISPLACED PERSONS

THE END OF THE WAR LEFT MANY PEOPLE SCATTERED ACROSS EUROPE, FAR FROM THEIR ORIGINAL HOMES. PERHAPS AS MANY AS 20 MILLION PEOPLE WERE UPROOTED DURING THE CONFLICT.

They included people who had been sent to Nazi concentration or forced labor camps, prisoners of war, and refugees from fighting and bombing, including Germans. As the war ended, many Germans feared the advance of the Soviet army and fled westward. There was chaos and desperation throughout Europe.

Refugees follow rail tracks from Lodz, in Poland, toward Berlin in the hope of being picked up by a train.

NOWHERE TO RUN

Many displaced persons (DPs) were separated from their families or had no families left at all. They lacked official papers or passports. Some were suffering from what is now called post-traumatic stress disorder, a state of shock experienced by people who have witnessed terrifying events. Some had lasting health problems, such as **tuberculosis** (TB).

UNITED NATIONS HELP

As early as 1943, a United Nations Relief and Rehabilitation Administration (UNRRA) had been planned, even though the United Nations Organization was not formally founded until after the war. The UNRRA set up camps for displaced persons in Italy, Austria, and Germany. It helped to trace families and organize **repatriation** (returning home). The camps were supported by the Allied military, by Christian and Jewish relief organizations, and by the Red Cross.

Jewish orphans, whose parents were killed during the war, at a children's center in Germany.

Members of the football team at the Berlin Displaced Persons Camp with US army officers.

A Jewish girl, Ursula Pluta, is photographed in an attempt to find her surviving relatives. Photographs like this were published in newspapers.

NEW BEGINNINGS

DP camp residents set up schools, universities, synagogues, churches, and social and sporting activities. These helped people to cope with their changing world. New friendships and even marriages were made. Over 250,000 Jews were in these camps between 1945 and 1952. Föhrenwald, in Bavaria, later run by the West German government, stayed open until 1957. Wels, in Austria, held DPs until 1959.

DESTINATIONS

SOME OF EUROPE'S DISPLACED PERSONS COULD NOT RETURN TO THEIR FORMER HOMES BECAUSE THEY WERE TOO SICK OR DISABLED, OR WERE PREVENTED BY POLITICAL CHANGES THAT HAD TAKEN PLACE AFTER THE WAR. Some refused to return to their homes, since they had bad memories of violence or persecution. Most countries had strict quotas for allowing in new immigrants and were slow to take action. Sometimes there was political opposition, too.

NEW HOMES, NEW LANDS

Over the years following the war, the rules were changed, and more displaced persons did find new homes and jobs in Western European countries such as the UK, France, and Belgium, and also in South America, Australia, and Canada. The USA took in about 400,000 refugees and displaced persons from Central and Eastern Europe, including 137,450 Jews. Many other Jews in the DP camps could not see a future for themselves in Europe and were encouraged by Zionist organizations to go to Palestine.

A sign for a Jewish barber shop in New York City in the 1940s.

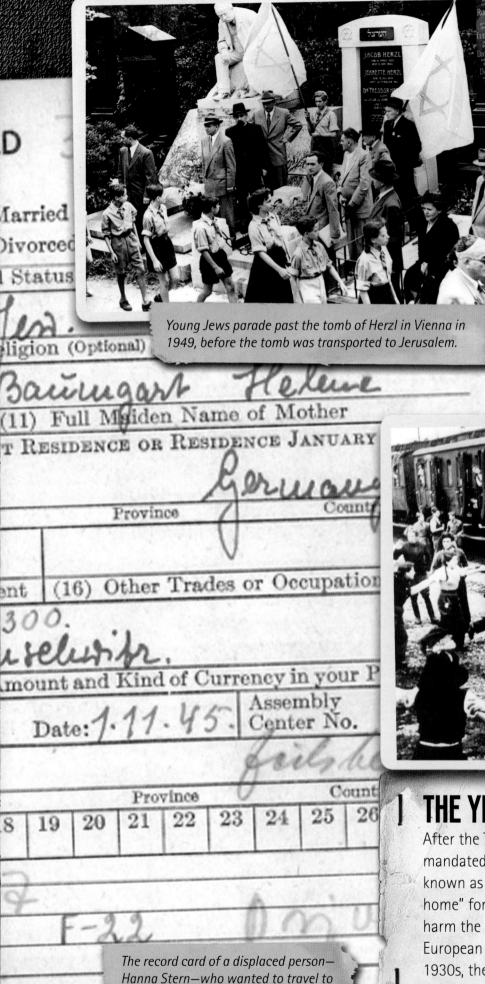

D 3

Married

Divorced

l Status

les?.

eligion (Optional)

Baumgart Helene

(11) Full Maiden Name of Mother

t RESIDENCE OR RESIDENCE JANUARY

Germa...

Province   Count...

ent   (16) Other Trades or Occupation...

300.

useweif.

mount and Kind of Currency in your P...

Date: 1.11.45.   Assembly Center No.

fritzh...

                    Province   Count...
8 | 19 | 20 | 21 | 22 | 23 | 24 | 25 | 26

F-22

The record card of a displaced person— Hanna Stern—who wanted to travel to the USA. It was issued in 1945.

ZIONISM

Zionism is a Jewish nationalist movement. It was founded in Europe in the nineteenth century by Theodor Herzl. He wanted to create a modern Jewish nation, preferably in the region where the historical land of Israel had once existed. The Zionists' plan was to offer Jews from the diaspora a place to escape from persecution. In Herzl's day the region, called Palestine, was ruled by the Ottoman Empire. Most of the population was Arab (both Muslim and Christian), and there was also a small Jewish population. Zionism steadily gained support among Jews, especially those from Eastern Europe.

Young Jews parade past the tomb of Herzl in Vienna in 1949, before the tomb was transported to Jerusalem.

Jewish refugees from DP camps dance at Munich station, Germany, before traveling to Palestine.

THE YISHUV

After the Turks were defeated in World War I, the League of Nations mandated (authorized) the United Kingdom to govern this region, known as Palestine. In 1917, the British had agreed to favor "a national home" for the Jewish people in Palestine, provided that it did not harm the rights of the Palestinians living there. A growing number of European Jews moved to Palestine between the two world wars. By the 1930s, the *Yishuv* (Jewish settlement in Palestine) numbered about 400,000. After the horrors of the Holocaust, many European Jews decided to follow their example, and they too set out for Palestine.

יציאת אירופה ת

ALIYAH BET

After the Holocaust, many European Jews sought a new home in British-ruled Palestine. Arabs in Palestine and the Middle East were against Zionist settlement and any partition (dividing) of the land. The British quotas for **immigration** were limited, so many displaced Jews tried to enter Palestine unofficially, by ship. This was known in Hebrew as the *Aliyah Bet*. The British tried to prevent it taking place because there was growing violence between the Arab population and the Jewish settlers. Both sides attacked the British. In 1947, the UK declared it would end the mandate and let the United Nations (which had now replaced the League of Nations) decide Palestine's future. The UN agreed upon a plan to partition the country, against the wishes of the Arabs.

THE STATE OF ISRAEL

ISRAEL DECLARED ITSELF AN **INDEPENDENT** NATION ON MAY 14, 1948. AS IT CAME INTO BEING, A WAR WAS BREAKING OUT BETWEEN ARAB COUNTRIES THAT OPPOSED THE PARTITION OF PALESTINE AND THE NEW STATE OF ISRAEL.

Israeli Jews called this period the "War of Independence," while Palestinian Arabs called it the *Nakbah*, or "Catastrophe." The Israeli forces won the war and extended Jewish territory. Many Palestinian Arabs were driven from their homes or fled the fighting. They then became refugees themselves.

First Israeli prime minister David Ben-Gurion reads out the proclamation of the State of Israel in 1948.

WAR OR PEACE?

Israel rapidly developed as a modern nation, with farms, factories, and cities. Its chief ally was the USA, and its armed forces became powerful. Further wars followed and there is still conflict across the region today as new Jewish settlements have been built on the Palestinian territory known as the West Bank. The settlers claim this land too as part of Israel, but the Palestinians want recognition as a nation in their own right. Both sides need peace, justice, and security, but few can agree on how to bring this about.

A view of Jerusalem, showing Christian, Muslim, and Jewish religious buildings in the foreground and skyscrapers in the distance.

82

THE PEOPLE OF ISRAEL

Israel today has a population of about 8 million. Jews make up about 75 percent of this, while most of the others are Arabs. Since 1948 Jews have been invited to settle in Israel from all over the diaspora. They have included many who were personally affected by the Holocaust, either as survivors or as relatives of those who suffered in the camps. Memories of the Holocaust have shaped almost every aspect of life in modern Israel.

Jewish and Arab children play together in a school in Jerusalem. Both Hebrew and Arabic letters are on the wall behind them.

SEEKING OUT THE TRUTH

Israel has played an important part in researching the histories of those who suffered in the Holocaust. Researchers have traced families and helped them to make contact with one another. They have helped to find family possessions and art treasures looted by the Nazis. They have tracked down surviving Nazi war criminals and helped bring them to trial. As more than 70 years have now passed since the Holocaust ended, there are fewer and fewer survivors who can describe their experience firsthand.

The flag of Israel features a large blue Star of David, an ancient Jewish symbol.

The Hall of Names at the Yad Vashem Museum, Jerusalem, Israel. There is also a computer center here where visitors can search a Holocaust victim database.

REMEMBRANCE

IN 1953, ISRAEL CREATED A NATIONAL HOLOCAUST REMEMBRANCE DAY, KNOWN IN HEBREW AS *YOM HASHOAH*. IN 2005, THE UNITED NATIONS GENERAL ASSEMBLY AGREED TO MAKE JANUARY 27 AN INTERNATIONAL HOLOCAUST REMEMBRANCE DAY. THIS DATE MARKS THE ANNIVERSARY OF THE LIBERATION OF THE AUSCHWITZ-BIRKENAU DEATH CAMP IN 1945.

There are public Holocaust memorials in cities around the world, from Australia to Canada. Memorials are places where public ceremonies can be held to honor the dead, or where individuals can visit and spend time reflecting and remembering.

STUMBLING BLOCKS

Another kind of memorial was invented by a German artist named Gunter Demnig. The *Stolperstein* (meaning "stumbling block") is the size of a cobblestone and records the details of an individual victim of the Nazis. It is set into the pavement in front of the person's former home or workplace. Each stone gives passersby a sudden reminder of the past. Since 1992, tens of thousands of these blocks have been placed in Germany and in other countries occupied by the Nazis.

Stolperstein *cobblestone memorial plaques in the Wilmersdorf district of Berlin, Germany.*

Israeli soldiers and the Israeli prime minster (center) lead the March of the Living commemorative march at Auschwitz on Holocaust Remembrance Day in 1998.

VISITING THE PAST

Visiting places associated with the Holocaust can provide a fresh understanding. Over a million people each year from all over the world visit the Anne Frank House in Amsterdam, the Netherlands (see page 40), which includes an exhibition about persecution and discrimination. Over 1.5 million people each year visit the site of Auschwitz, in Poland. In many countries there are organizations, museums, and schools that teach young people about the Holocaust and the issues it raises.

THE MESSAGE

Another way of educating people about the past is through the arts. Music, art, film, dance, theater, and books written for both adults and children have all approached the difficult and painful subject of the Holocaust. As the years pass, commemorating what happened is still as important as ever. It informs new generations, and it may comfort older people to think about and remember their loved ones.

The Book Thief is a book by Markus Zusak about a girl living in Germany during the Nazi regime. Her family hides a Jewish man in their home. The book was made into a film in 2013.

This Holocaust Memorial in a public park in Harrisburg, Pennsylvania, was designed by David Ascalon.

BERLIN, 60 YEARS LATER . . .

On May 10, 2005, 60 years after the end of World War II, a huge memorial was opened in the heart of Berlin, Germany, near the Brandenburg Gate. It was the work of American architect Peter Eisenman, and was named the "Memorial to the Murdered Jews of Europe." It is made up of 2,711 plain concrete slabs of different heights. Children play hide-and-seek between them. Tourists peer down the rows or walk into the depths until they can no longer see their way out. Snow, autumn leaves, and summer sunlight change the memorial's appearance. Underneath the memorial is a Learning Center with the names of Jews who died in the Holocaust.

NEVER AGAIN

THE BEST POSSIBLE MEMORIAL TO THE MILLIONS WHO DIED IN THE HOLOCAUST WOULD BE TO STOP SUCH A TRAGEDY FROM EVER HAPPENING AGAIN. WE ALL HAVE TO BUILD SOCIETIES BASED ON HUMANITY, RESPECT, AND COMMUNITY.

This involves individuals being prepared to speak out loudly and clearly against injustice, even when most people are keeping silent. It's also about finding ways to end conflict and division between peoples and to work together. Finally, it means offering a safe refuge to victims of war and persecution.

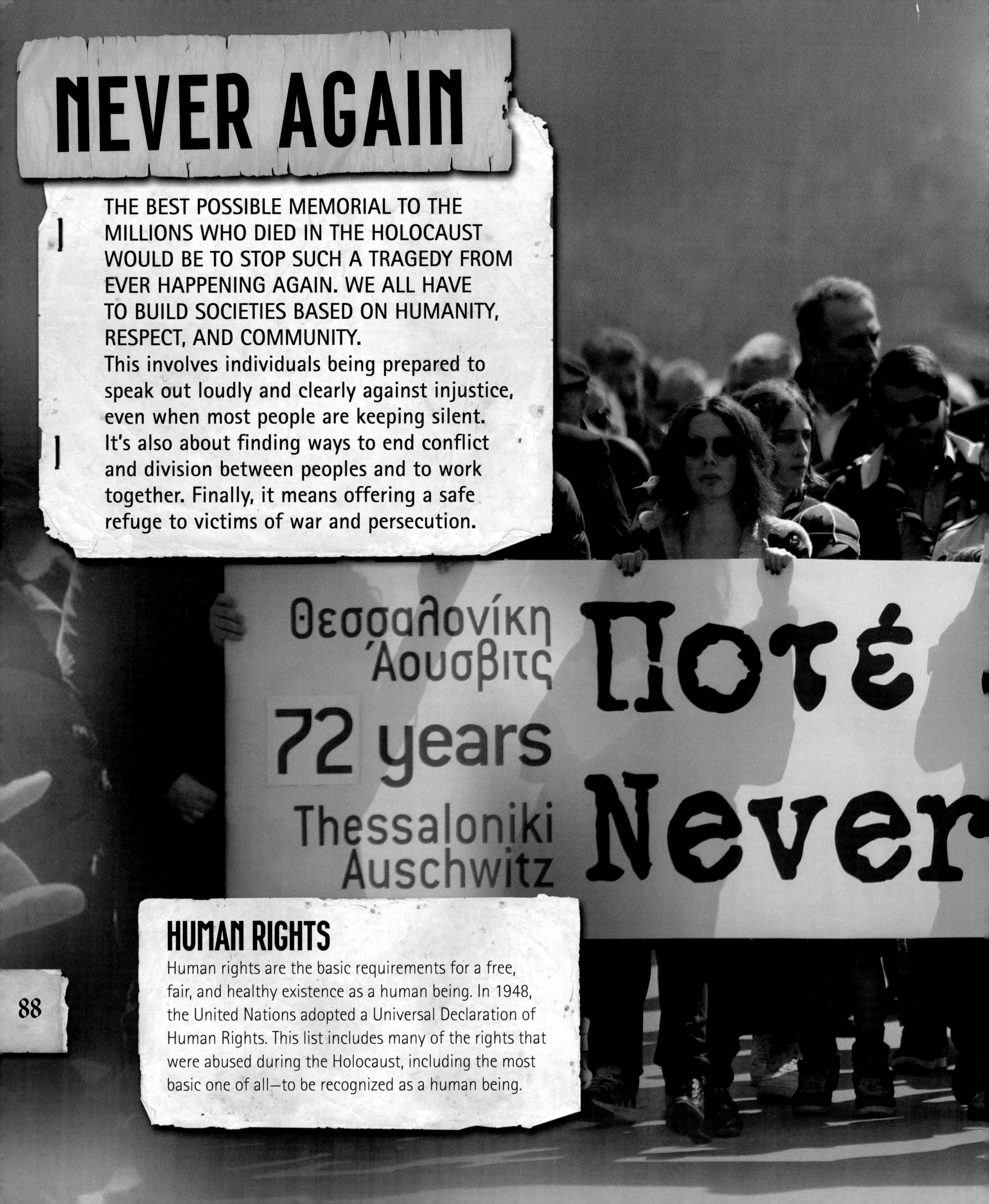

Θεσσαλονίκη
Άουσβιτς
72 years
Thessaloniki
Auschwitz

Ποτέ
Never

HUMAN RIGHTS

Human rights are the basic requirements for a free, fair, and healthy existence as a human being. In 1948, the United Nations adopted a Universal Declaration of Human Rights. This list includes many of the rights that were abused during the Holocaust, including the most basic one of all—to be recognized as a human being.

A protester in an anti-fascist rally in London, in July 2015.

REMEMBER AND LEARN

The 21st century has seen warfare, terrorism, growing religious intolerance, and racism, including antisemitism. Many governments place trade or military alliances above the basic principles of human rights. New fascist parties have won votes in many parts of the world and some of them even deny that the Holocaust ever happened. The facts of the Holocaust must be learned and remembered so that nothing like it can ever happen again.

A Dutch Holocaust survivor and childhood friend of Anne Frank, Hanneli Pick-Goslar, visits an exhibition about Anne Frank in Amsterdam, in 2012.

ξανά!
again!

ΔΗΜΟΣ ΘΕΣΣΑΛΟΝΙΚΗΣ
CITY OF THESSALONIKI

A Holocaust remembrance march in Thessaloniki, Greece, in 2015. Jews were transported from Thessaloniki to Auschwitz during the Holocaust.

"Look at how a single candle can both defy and define the darkness."

Anne Frank, 1929-1945
Diarist and writer, and victim of
the Holocaust

GLOSSARY

Antisemitic
Hating Jews, or discriminating against them.

Atomic bomb
A bomb with massive destructive power, created by splitting the atom.

Capitalist
Belonging to an economic system that is based on the private ownership of production, on competing markets, and on making profit.

Charismatic
Having a strong personality that can influence others or attract followers.

Civil rights
The basic rights of everyone in society, regardless of sex, race, or religion.

Collaborator
During a war, someone who cooperates with the enemy.

Commonwealth
An international treaty organization, founded in 1926 as the British Commonwealth. Today it is called the Commonweath of Nations.

Communism/Communist
The theory of a society in which property and methods of production are owned and controlled by the community. Its supporters are called communists.

Concentration camp
A center where a government imprisons large numbers of people, often without trial.

Consul
An official who lives in a foreign country and looks after the interests of people living there from his or her own country.

Crematorium (plural: crematoria)
A place where dead bodies are burned in a furnace.

Culture
A way of life within a social group, especially one that enjoys civilized skills such as art, music, literature, and science.

Dehumanize
To treat someone as if he or she is not human and remove their personality, feelings, and independence.

Democratic
Belonging to a political system in which government and law are controlled by the citizens or by their elected representatives.

De-Nazification
A program of reforms brought in to Germany by the Allies after World War II. Nazis were removed from powerful positions. Anti-Jewish laws were abolished.

Deportation
The enforced removal of people from one place to another.

Diaspora
Any population that has become scattered across many countries.

Dictator
A ruler who has total power and is not elected by the people.

Diplomat
A government official who represents his or her country abroad, negotiating agreements or handling international affairs.

Discrimination
To make a distinction between people, in favor of one group or against another. It can form a part of racist behavior.

Displaced person
A person removed from his or her homeland by deportation, war, or natural disaster.

Eugenics
Methods of improving the "quality" of the human race, for example by encouraging or preventing the breeding of certain groups of people. Nazi eugenics were based on meaningless theories of "racial purity" and cruel persecution of the disabled.

Extermination camp
A concentration camp used as a center for organized mass murder.

Fascist
Following an extreme nationalist and militarist political movement that started in Italy during World War I. Similar movements are also sometimes called "fascist."

Final Solution
The "final solution to the Jewish question" was the term used by the Nazi leadership to describe their plan for exterminating Jews.

Genocide
The organized extermination of a group of people.

Ghetto
Ghettos were originally city districts in medieval Europe where Jews were forced to live. In Nazi Germany, ghettos were used to segregate Jews and organize their deportation to camps.

Holocaust
The persecution and murder of about 6 million Jews, organized by the Nazis during the 1930s and 40s. An additional 5 million people were killed, including Roma, Slavs, and Soviet prisoners of war.

Human rights
The basic needs that must be met for a human being to live a healthy and happy life, such as shelter, education, health care, freedom, equality, and justice.

Humanitarian
Dedicated to saving life or preventing suffering.

Immigration
The movement of people from one country into another.

Independent
Of a nation; self-ruling.

Inflation
A rise in the cost of goods and services over a period of time.

Interned/internment
To be imprisoned or locked up without trial.

Intolerance
Refusing to respect the views or customs of other people.

Islam
The faith of Muslims, who believe that there is a single God (Allah) and that Muhammad was his Prophet.

Jehovah's Witnesses
A Christian group who are strongly opposed to war and resist state authority.

Judaism
The religion of the Jews, which declares that there is a single God, who revealed his laws to Moses on Mount Sinai.

Medieval
To do with the Middle Ages, a period of European history that lasted from the fifth to the fifteenth century.

Migration
Movement of people on a large scale, often caused by economic need, changing environment, or the need to escape war or persecution.

Mutiny
A rebellion by armed forces against their officers; a refusal to carry out orders.

Nationalist
1) Anyone seeking to create a new or independent nation.
2) Someone who glorifies his or her own nation, or believes that it is better than others.

Occupy
To invade and take control of another territory or nation.

Oppression
Using power in an unfair way that suppresses freedom.

Pacifist
Someone who is against all war and violence, as a matter of principle.

Partisan
A fighter who is not part of a regular army, who resists invasion or occupation by foreign troops.

Persecution
The cruel or oppressive treatment of people, often because of their race, their religion, or their political views.

Pogrom
A riot, attack, or massacre organized against an ethnic group, especially Jews living in the former Russian Empire.

Prisoners of war
Enemy soldiers captured in battle and often imprisoned in camps.

Propaganda
Information, often exaggerated or untrue, intended to help or harm a cause.

Race
A group of people identified by their shared characteristics, such as physical appearance or skin color. Most modern scientists believe that the term has little value, because it does not take into account genetic variation within such groups.

Racism/racist
Believing that humans can be divided into races, and that some of these are superior to others.

Refugee
Someone who has fled from his or her homeland because of war, persecution, or a natural disaster.

Regime
A government or period of rule.

Reparation
Payments made from one country to another, to make up for a wrongdoing.

Repatriation
Returning people to their own country.

Republic
A country that is ruled by a representative of the people, such as a president, rather than by an emperor, king, or queen.

Resistance fighter
One of a secret group fighting to free their country from foreign occupation.

Revolution
A sudden change in the way that a country is governed, often using force or violence.

Sabotage
Destroying machinery, power lines, or railway tracks as part of a political campaign.

Sanitation
The process for keeping places clean and free from disease, such as cleaning the streets and removing garbage.

Social justice
A social system that is responsible and treats people fairly.

Socialist
Supporting the political and economic theory that the production of goods and services should be publicly owned or regulated.

Soviet Union
The nations, including Russia, that formed the country called the Union of Soviet Socialist Republics (1922-1991). Also known as the USSR.

Swastika
A symbol of good luck dating back to prehistoric times in Asia and other parts of the world. The Nazis chose a reversed version of it as their symbol.

Transit camp
A type of concentration camp in which prisoners were held before being sent on to labor or extermination camps.

Tuberculosis
An infectious disease of the lungs, also known as TB or consumption.

Typhus
Any of several severe fevers caused by deadly bacteria.

Zionism
A political movement founded by nationalist Jews in the 19th century. It campaigned for settlement by Jews in their ancient homeland and the creation of a Jewish nation-state.

INDEX

PICTURE CREDITS

The publishers would like to thank the following sources for their kind permission to reproduce the pictures in this book.
Key: t = top, b = bottom, l = left, r = right, c= center

This edition published by Scholastic Inc., 557 Broadway, New York NY 10012

Text, design, and illustrations © 2016 Carlton Books Limited. All rights reserved.

This edition published in the United States by Scholastic Inc. September 2016

Hardback: ISBN 978-1-338-03040-2
Paperback: ISBN 978-0-545-93319-3

10 9 8 7 6 5 4 3 2 1

Printed in China

Historical Consultant: Dan Stone, Professor of Modern History, Royal Holloway, University of London

Executive Editor: Selina Wood
Art Editor: Dani Lurie
Design: Wildpixel Ltd.
Picture Research: Steve Behan
Production: Lisa Cook